Puffin Books
Making Rubik's Magic™

This book tells you how to solve Rubik's Magic™, the intriguing new brain-teaser from the master of manipulation. More than that, it describes some Quick Tricks with which to amaze your friends and illustrates over fifty different interesting shapes that can be made with the puzzle. Solving the problem is only the first step to the hours of fun which this book will provide.

Albie Fiore studied architecture at Southend School of Architecture and the Architectural Association in London. After some years as an architect, he worked as a chef on private yachts in the Mediterranean, ran an antique business specializing in old penny-arcade slot machines, of which he has a collection, and later became editor of *Games and Puzzles* magazine. He spent several years as production editor of *White Dwarf* magazine and as production manager and product designer for a games company. He has also written *Shaping Rubik's Snake*™ and *Unscrupulous?*, both published by Penguin.

He has recently co-founded Hatch, a design and production group.

Albie Fiore

MAKING RUBIK'S MAGIC™

Devised and produced by **HATCH**

Puffin Books

Puffin Books, Penguin Books Ltd, Harmondsworth, Middlesex, England
Viking Penguin Inc., 40 West 23rd Street, New York, New York 10010, U.S.A.
Penguin Books Australia Ltd, Ringwood, Victoria, Australia
Penguin Books Canada Limited, 2801 John Street, Markham, Ontario, Canada L3R 1B4
Penguin Books (N.Z.) Ltd, 182-190 Wairau Road, Auckland 10, New Zealand

First published 1986

Designed by Bowden Van Amerongen

Made and printed in Great Britain by
Richard Clay (The Chaucer Press) Ltd, Bungay, Suffolk
Filmset in Rockwell by Rowland Phototypesetting (London) Ltd

To Simon,
The Sudan, Sunshine and Surprises

CONTENTS

Introduction   9
1   The Making of Magic   10
2   The Puzzle   14
3   Basic Moves   16
4   Solving the Puzzle   30
5   Quick Tricks   36
6   Easy Shapes   42
7   Difficult Shapes   55

INTRODUCTION

Rubik's Magic™ was invented by, surprise, surprise, Professor Ernö Rubik. This Hungarian sculptor, designer and architectural engineer is already a household name, thanks to his other inventions in the game and puzzle field: Rubik's Cube™ and Rubik's Snake™.

Whereas the Cube was an infuriatingly difficult puzzle and the Snake was a shape-making exercise, Rubik's Magic™ is an elegant combination of the two. It is both a puzzle and a shape-making game.

The intention of this book is to show you the scope of this plaything and, if necessary, to provide you with the solution to the puzzle. After reading it through and trying the problems posed, you will find that you too can do magic.

1 THE MAKING OF MAGIC

Rubik's Magic™ comprises eight squares. The squares are bound together by four loops of nylon, which spiral around them. When flat, the loops are as shown in Figure 1.

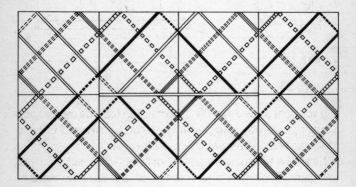

Figure 1

The effect of these loops is to form two-way hinges between the squares. When folded and opened correctly, the nylon will transfer from one square to the other, moving the hinge through 90° in the process. This is the same principle as that involved in the Chinese Wallet, a children's toy.

In the wallet, however, the hinge transfers from one side of the square to the side directly opposite. In Rubik's Magic™, because the nylon cord crosses the square at 45°, the hinge transfers to an adjacent side. You will be able to see this more clearly by making two small models.

To make the Chinese Wallet, take two squares of different-coloured cardboard and join them as shown in Figure 2. It is best to use two different-coloured sets of ribbon as the hinges. The ends should be stuck down as indicated.

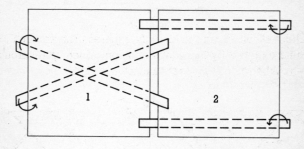

Figure 2

If you now close the wallet, you will find that you can reopen it the opposite way, and you will see that the coloured ribbons have transferred from one square to the other.

Now take two more squares of different-coloured card and two pairs of coloured ribbon as before, but this time connect them as shown in Figure 3.

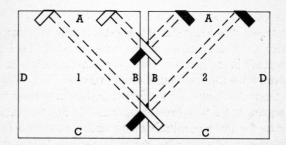

Figure 3

This is how the squares in Rubik's Magic™ are connected. If you fold them, you will find that they reopen in a different way. Figure 4a shows the model as you made it, while Figure 4b shows the model after you have closed it and reopened it the other way. Once again the ribbons have transferred from one square to the other. Also the squares were initially hinged along the edges marked B, but after folding and reopening they are now hinged along the edges marked A.

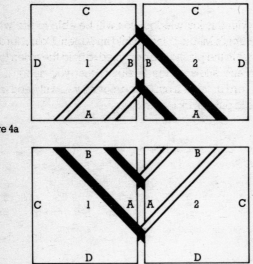

Figure 4a

Figure 4b

Because Rubik's Magic™ has four separate cords running across each square, the common hinged side can be moved all around each square. However, if you label any two adjacent squares as shown in Figure 5, side A on one will always hinge with side A on the other, side B with B, side C with C, and side D with D.

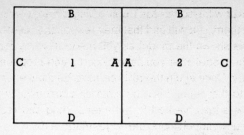

Figure 5

Armed with this knowledge, you will be able to see which way your Rubik's Magic™ should fold and open. Do not force it. The grooves in the plastic are designed to hold the nylon loops in position and allow all the flexibility that you need. If you break the cord or force it out of its grooves, you will need more than magic to put it back together again.

2 THE PUZZLE

On one side of Rubik's Magic™ is a printed pattern of three separate coloured rings. On the reverse is another printed pattern of three linked rings.

To commence the puzzle, you must first make the three separate rings (as shown in Figure 6) from the pattern in which you bought the puzzle.

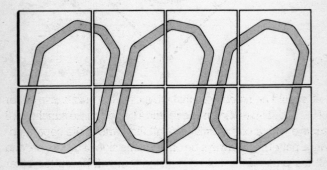

Figure 6

The puzzle is to transform the rectangle into the shape shown in Figure 7, so that the pattern of the three linked rings on the reverse side is formed.

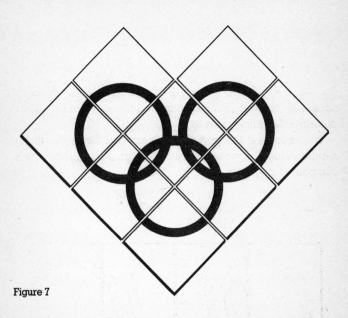

Figure 7

It should be noted here that whenever the puzzle is in either of the two shapes shown above (the 4 x 2 rectangle and the 3 x 3 square with a corner missing), all the parts of the separated-rings pattern will always be on the same side of the shape, and all the parts of the linked-rings pattern will be on the other side.

The next chapter describes some simple folds that will help you to solve the puzzle. The actual solution is given later in the book, but look there only as a last resort. If you are feeling adventurous, you should try solving it before reading any further; it isn't too difficult. But try to avoid any three-dimensional shapes at the moment, as some of these are very difficult to get out of, and the hints in the next chapter all presume that the puzzle is still in a 4 x 2 rectangle.

3 BASIC MOVES

The following moves are very simple and should be learnt well. They are an essential part of solving the puzzle and will prove helpful in making many of the shapes later in the book.

For all these moves it is necessary only that the puzzle start as a 4 x 2 rectangle. The separated-rings pattern need not have been formed. However, if the puzzle will not fold and open as shown, it means that the first rectangle was the wrong way up. Turn the puzzle over so that the surface that was on top is now underneath.

The Reverse

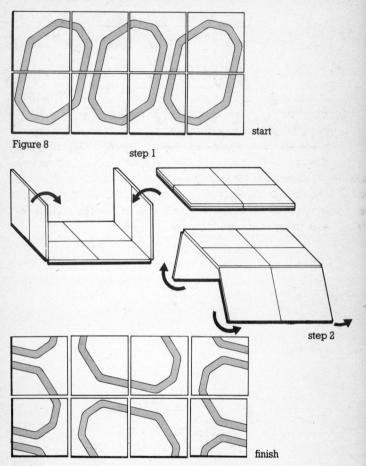

Figure 8

start

step 1

step 2

finish

Fold the two ends up and in, as shown in step 1. Then peel out the two sections on the underside, as in step 2. Turn over to the separated-rings side. If you repeat the process from step 1 with the same side uppermost, it will return the puzzle to the pattern you started with.

The Concertina

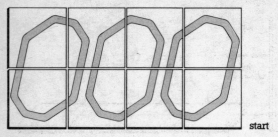

Figure 9

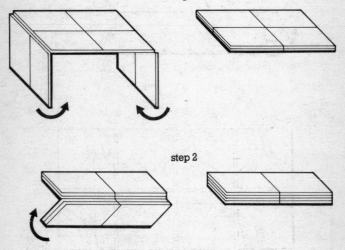

step 1

step 2

start

Fold the two ends down and under, as shown in step 1. Then fold the half nearest you down and under to form a four-deep stack, as in step 2. Grip the centres of the edges of the top and bottom layers and pull outwards. The whole thing will

18

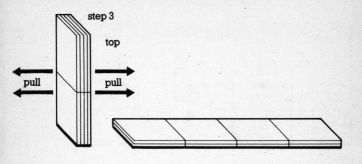

step 3

top

pull

pull

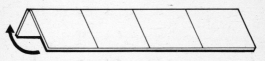

step 4

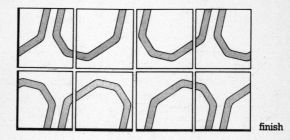

finish

concertina out into a flat strip. Open this up by folding the underside down and out. You can return to your initial pattern by starting from step 1 again, but you must first turn your final pattern face-down.

The Roll

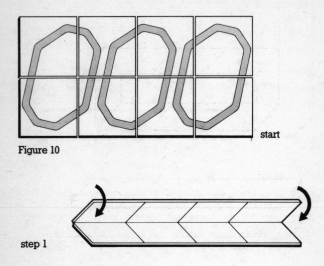

Figure 10

start

step 1

Fold the rectangle in half by swinging the edge furthest from you up and over, as in step 1. Grip the top layer on either side of the first hinge in from the right and the underside by the first from the left. With your right hand pull up and out, as in step 2. The strip will roll along one square. Open up by swinging the top layer towards you. At step 2 you can roll to the left or even grip two hinges in from each end. If you keep rolling, you will come back to your starting pattern. However, you will find that sometimes the rectangle must be folded the other way at steps 1 and 3.

If you open the roll out at step 2, the squares will all be linked, edge to edge, in a ring. In this configuration it is easy to see that the eight squares of the puzzle are joined by spiralling nylon loops.

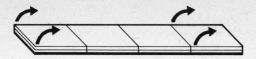

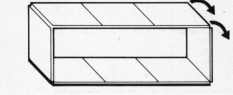

step 2

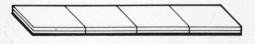

step 3

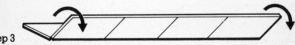

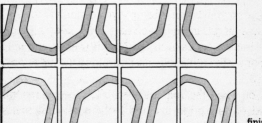

finish

The Windmill

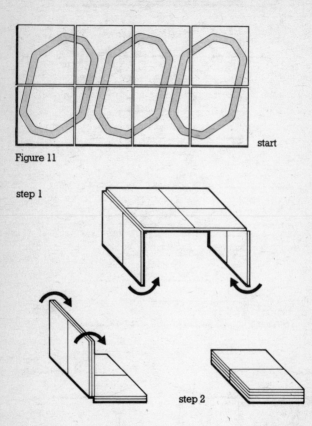

start

Figure 11

step 1

step 2

Fold the two outer edges down and under, as in step 1. Then fold the left-hand half up and over to make a four-deep stack. Now peel the top right leaf down and the bottom left leaf up, as shown in step 3. Fold the two outer sections down and pull them apart, as in steps 4 and 5. The puzzle will fold out into a rectangle again.

During the windmill action at step 3, you can, in fact, peel

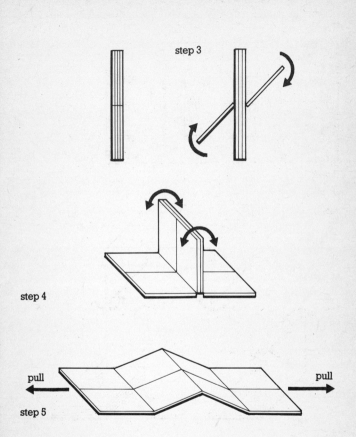

step 3

step 4

pull   pull

step 5

down as many leaves as you wish from either left or right as long as you peel up the same number from the opposite lower half, so that there are four on top and four below. If you open out at each stage, you will discover several different patterns. If you repeat the windmill action one leaf at a time, you will return to your starting pattern.

Patterned Rectangles

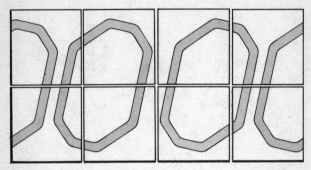

Figure 12

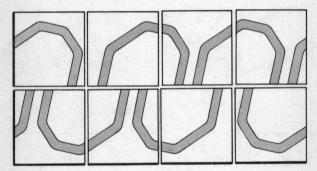

Figure 13

The side with the separated rings can be transformed into
many different patterns. All fit the 4 x 2 rectangle and can be
made using only those sequences that have been described in

24

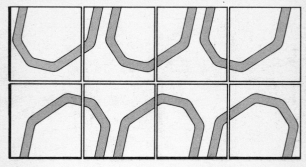

Figure 14

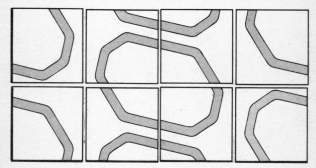

Figure 15

this chapter. On the next few pages you will find some of the patterns. As a useful exercise in practising the four basic sequences, try to make these patterns.

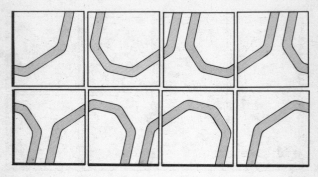

Figure 16

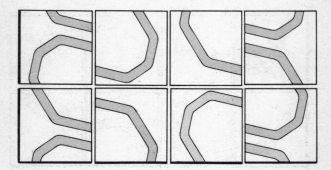

Figure 17

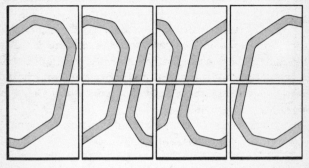

Figure 18

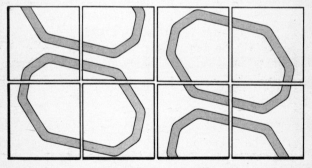

Figure 19

The Transformer

This is the most important sequence in solving the puzzle. It transforms the 4 x 2 rectangle into the 3 x 3 square with the corner missing.

In the diagram the starting position has the separated-rings pattern completed and on the underside. The sequence can be done from any initial 4 x 2 rectangle, but if yours will not follow the first two steps, then your initial rectangle should be turned over so that the side that was uppermost is now underneath.

Fold the right-hand end up and over, as in step 1. Swing the furthermost square of these two up and towards you, as in step 2. Swing the two top right-hand squares up and over into the middle, as in step 3. Now swing the middle and right-hand squares nearest you up and away from you, as in step 4. Swing the top central square furthest from you up and over on to the right-hand end, as in step 5. The top two squares will now swing up and away from you, as shown in step 6, to form the 3 x 3 square with the corner missing.

To return to the 4 x 2 rectangle, you must follow these steps in reverse.

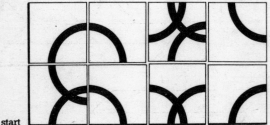

start

Figure 20

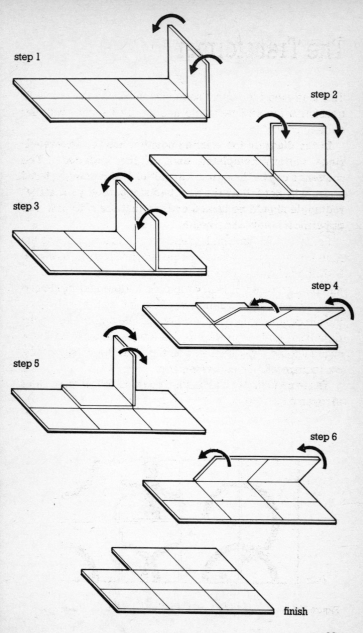

step 1

step 2

step 3

step 4

step 5

step 6

finish

29

4 SOLVING THE PUZZLE

The basic moves described in the previous chapter are all that you need to know to solve the puzzle.

If you have not yet solved it, now is the time to do so. Having mastered the basic moves, you should not find the problem too difficult.

To begin the solution, you must have the puzzle in a 4 x 2 rectangle with the separated-rings pattern made up. To do this, form the 4 x 2 rectangle and alternate the 'Reverse' sequence and 'Concertina' sequences. These will bring you to one of the following patterns:

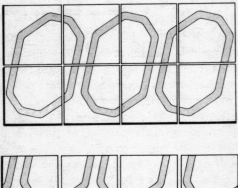

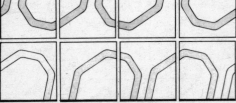

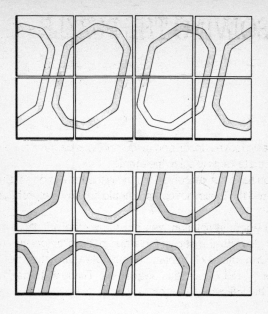

These last three can then be changed to the separated-rings pattern by simply using the 'Roll'. **Don't forget that if the puzzle will not fold as shown in the first few steps, the rectangle that you started from must be turned over so the face that was uppermost is now underneath.**

Having reached the starting position, you should now try to solve the puzzle yourself using the moves in the previous chapter. If, however, frustration gets the better of you, the solution is given on the following pages.

One way or another, you should become practised in solving the puzzle before going on to the tricks and shapes in the later chapters, as some of them may lead you into shapes that you will have difficulty unravelling.

The Solution

Start with the separated-rings pattern completed and face-up, as shown at the start of Figure 21.

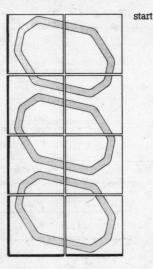

start

Figure 21

Fold the two end sections up and over, as shown in step 1. Then fold the two sections on the underside down and out, as in step 2. (This is the 'Reverse' sequence.)

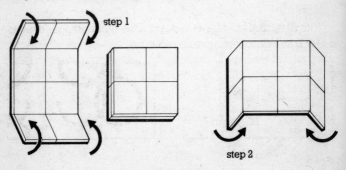

step 1

step 2

32

Fold the half nearer you down and under to form a two-deep 4 x 1 rectangle, as shown in step 3. Grip the first hinge in from the left of the top layer and the first in from the right on the bottom layer and roll the rectangle along one, as in step 4. Open up by lifting the top half up and away, as in step 5. (This is the 'Roll' sequence.)

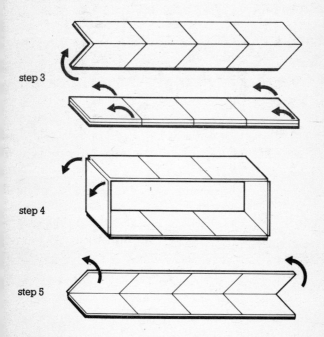

step 3

step 4

step 5

The pattern should be as in step 6. Turn the rectangle over to reveal the linked-rings side, as in step 6.

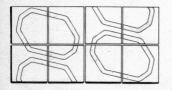

step 6

All you need to do now is follow the 'Transformer' sequence. Fold the right-hand end up and over, as in step 7. Then flip the top right-hand corner square up and over towards you, as in step 8.

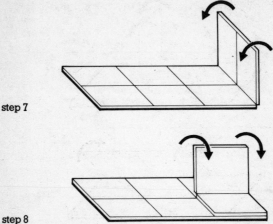

step 7

step 8

Fold the top two right-hand end sections up and in, as in step 9. Then fold the top centre section nearest you and the right side section up and over, as shown in step 10.

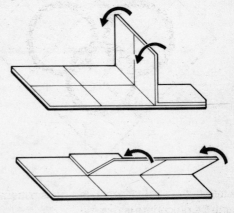

step 9

step 10

Fold the top centre section in the back row up and over on to the top right-hand corner, as in step 11. Then flip the top centre and top right sections on the far side up and over away from you, as in step 12. You will now have formed the completed linked-rings pattern.

step 11

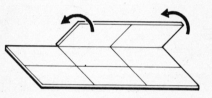

step 12

finish

To return to the original separated-rings pattern, you must go through the procedure in reverse.

5 QUICK TRICKS

This chapter describes some Quick Tricks. These are
three-dimensional shapes that you can make literally with a
flick of the wrist – a little bit of magic!

The Eight-Point Star

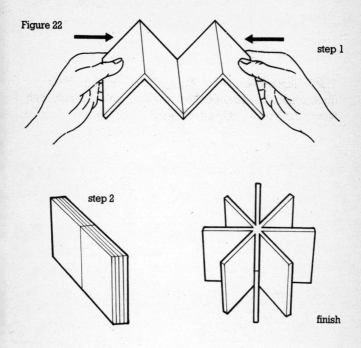

Figure 22

step 1

step 2

finish

Start with the separated-rings pattern completed and upper-most. Grip the ends of the puzzle, as shown in step 1, and push inwards so that the puzzle concertinas into a four-deep 4 x 1 stack, as in step 2. As you do this, ensure that the centre folds away from you. The arms of the stack can now be separated into the eight-pointed star shown as the finish. (This is in fact the 'Windmill' sequence described earlier.)

This and the other tricks in this section can be done from any initial 4 x 2 rectangle, but you may find that the folds need to be away from you instead of towards you, or vice versa, depending on your starting pattern.

The Tube

Figure 23

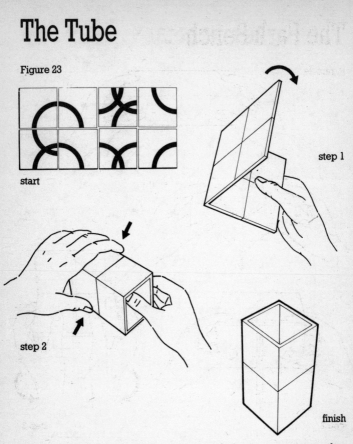

start

step 1

step 2

finish

Start with the completed separated-rings pattern on the underside. Grip the puzzle at one end, with your thumb down the centre fold on the top side. Swing the other half of the puzzle up and over on to your thumb, as in step 1. With your other hand grip the outer edges and squeeze in, as in step 2. With practice you will find that the puzzle will pop into the square tube shown as the finish.

The Park Bench

Figure 24

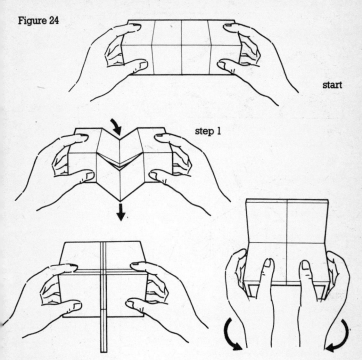

start

step 1

step 2

step 3

Start with the separated-rings pattern complete and upper-most. Grip the puzzle, as shown in the illustration of the starting position, so that the top half is folded away from you and is at right angles to the lower half. With one finger poke the centre two sections in the top half downwards and push the ends in, so that the puzzle concertinas, as shown in steps 1 and 2.

Still gripping the ends, swing your wrists together, as shown in step 3. The puzzle will take the shape of a park bench.

You can also perform this trick by pushing the top two centre sections upwards instead of down in step 1.

The Winged Cube

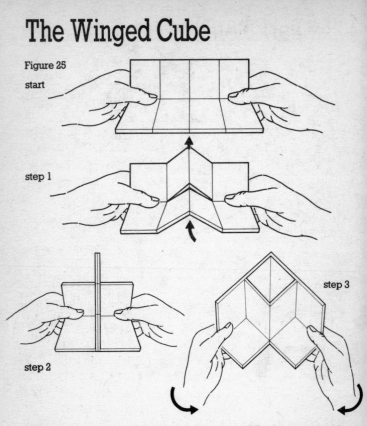

Figure 25

start

step 1

step 2

step 3

Start with the completed separated-rings side uppermost. As shown in the diagram, grip so that the rear half is folded upwards at right angles to the half nearer you. With one finger flick the centre two sections of the lower half upwards and push in, so that the centre two sections of the top half fold out, as in step 1. The puzzle should now be in the form shown in step 2.

Now swing your wrists towards each other. The puzzle will open out into the winged cube shown in step 3.

With a little practice you can go from this shape back to the rectangle and straight into the park bench described earlier or vice versa.

The M-Square

Figure 26

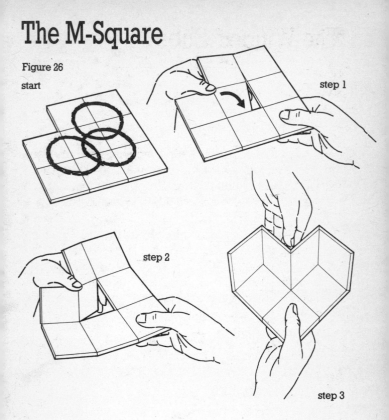

start

step 1

step 2

step 3

This Quick Trick starts with the linked-rings pattern completed and uppermost, as shown in the diagram. Grip the corner nearest you with one hand, and push inwards with the thumb of the other hand, so that the central square starts to tilt downwards. The corner of this should then be supported by the index finger, as shown in step 1.

Now swing the central square down and outwards, as shown in step 2. It will easily flap round to leave a 2 x 2 square with the M-shaped series of walls shown in step 3.

41

6 EASY SHAPES

The collection of shapes on the following pages can be made very easily, with just a few folds, from either the 4 x 2 rectangle or the 3 x 3 square with the corner missing.

Since this puzzle is quite difficult to manipulate into a required shape, you may find it more satisfying to experiment and tick off various shapes as you learn how to make them.

No solutions are provided for any of the shapes in this chapter or the next, as it would take a much longer book to record all the necessary moves. There are over fifty shapes that can be formed in these last two chapters, and I wish you many enjoyable hours of magic as you discover them all as well as inventing some new ones of your own.

1

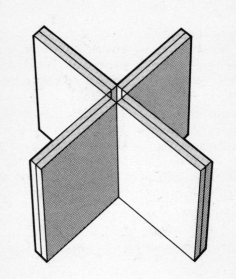

2

44

3

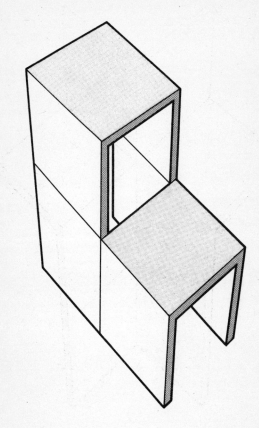

4

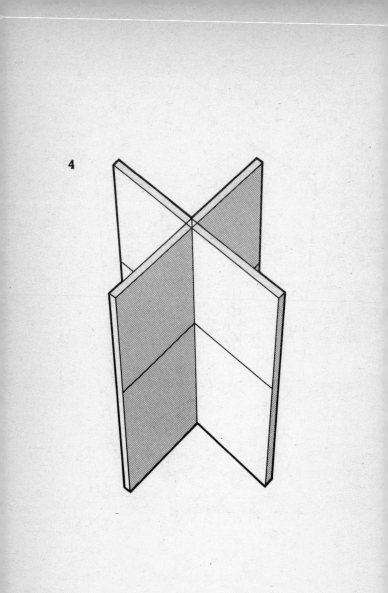

5

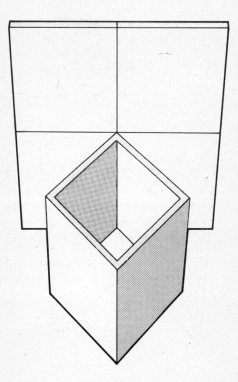

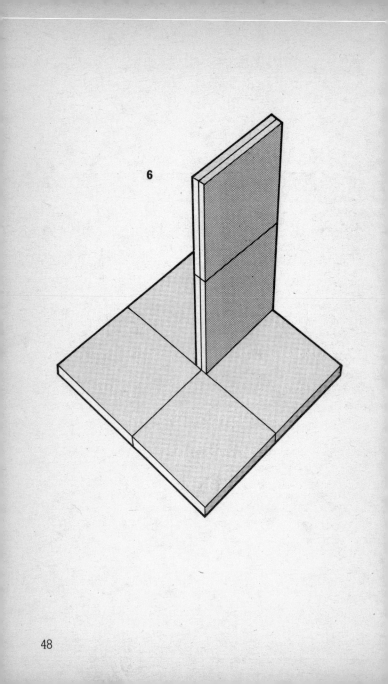

6

48

7

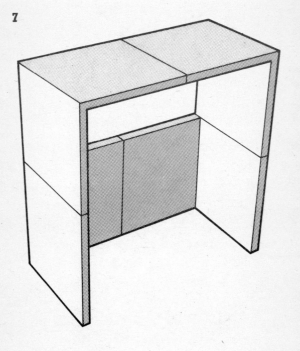

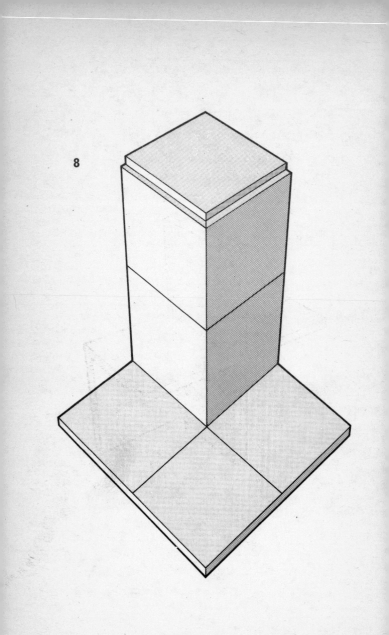

8

9

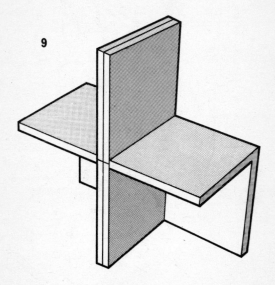

10

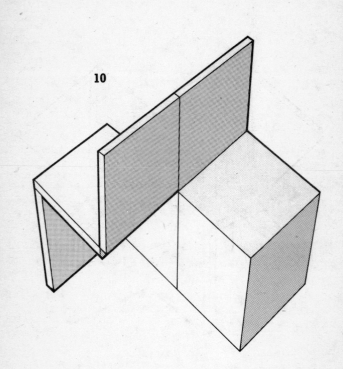

11

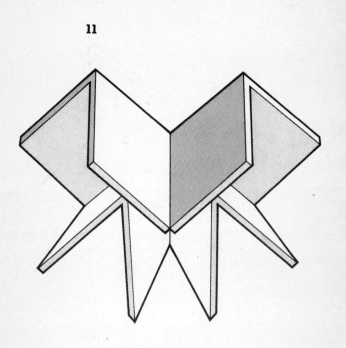

12

7 DIFFICULT SHAPES

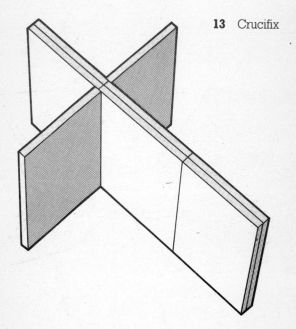

13 Crucifix

14

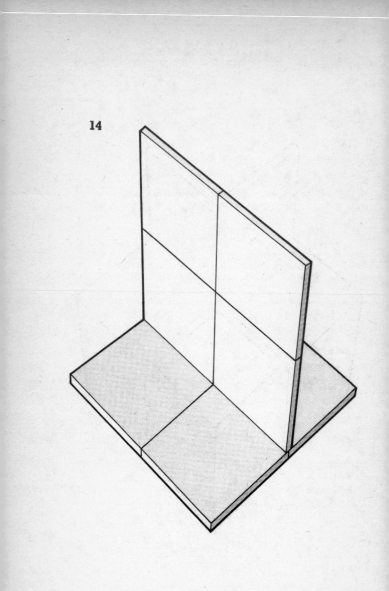

15

16

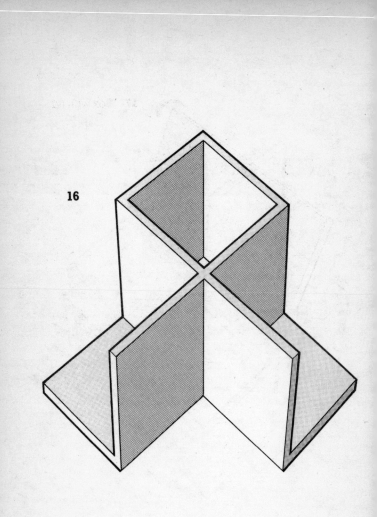

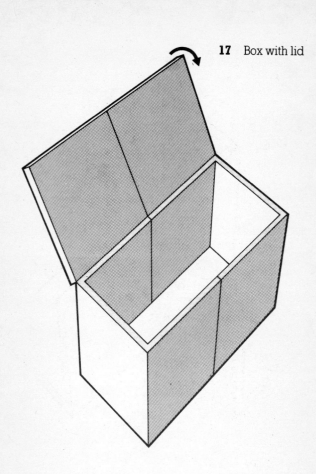

17 Box with lid

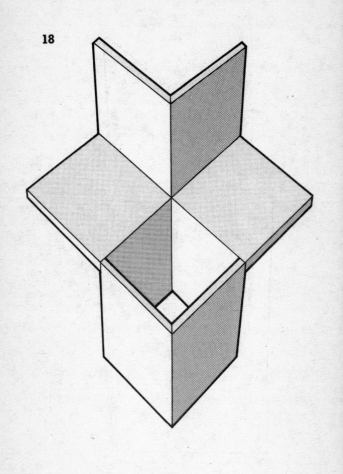

19

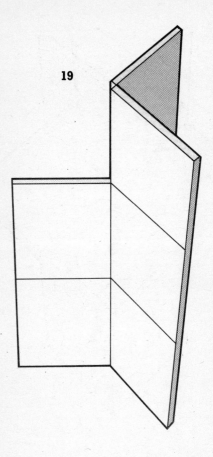

20 Sofa

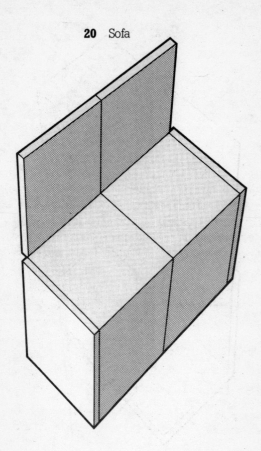

21

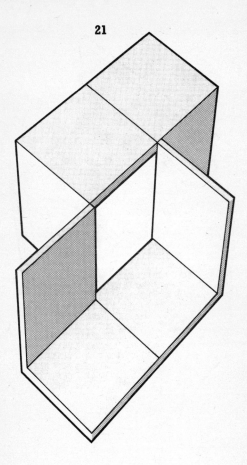

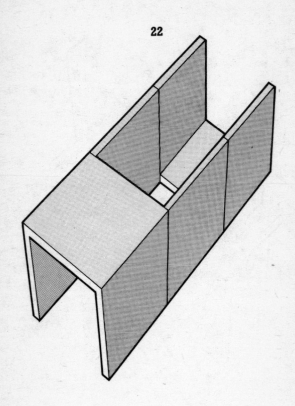

22

23

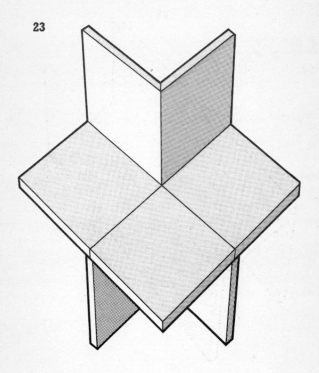

24

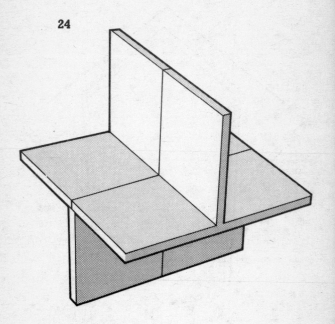

25

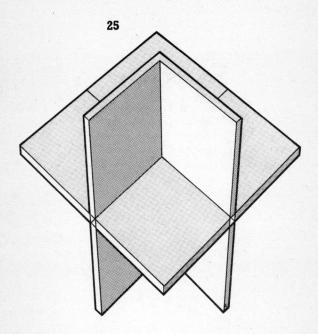

26 Chalet

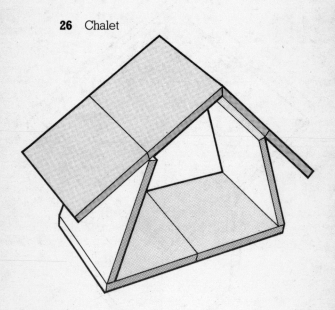

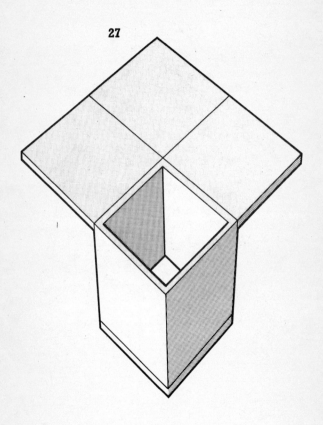

27

28

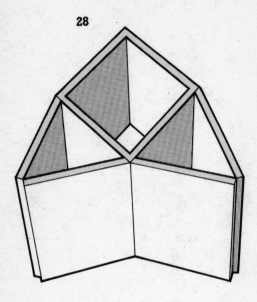

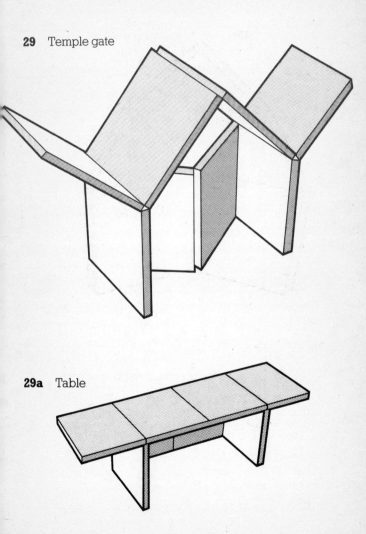

29 Temple gate

29a Table

30 Staggered hinge

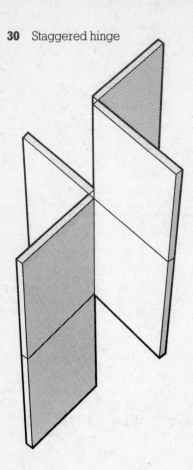

31

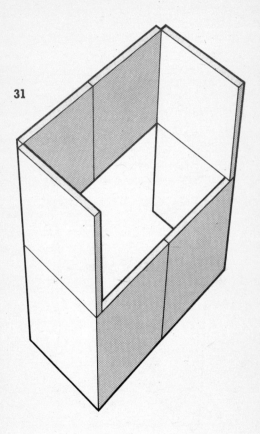

32

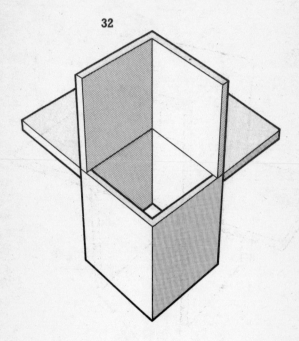

33

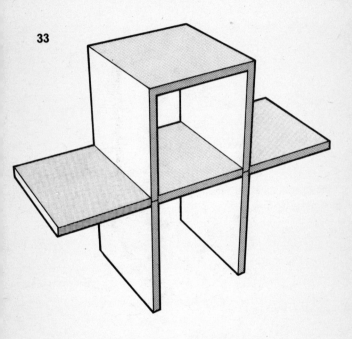

34

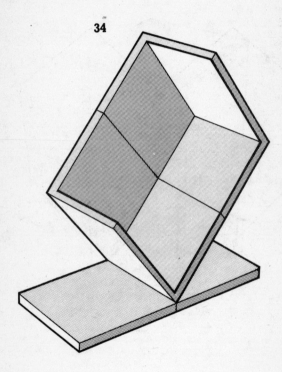

35

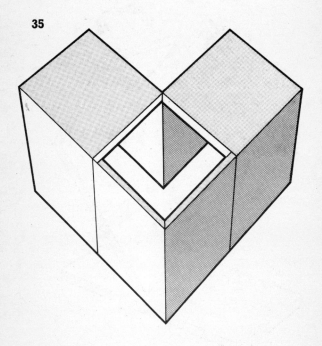

36

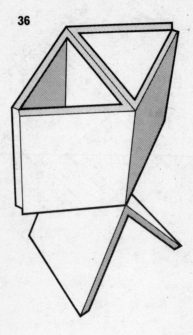

37

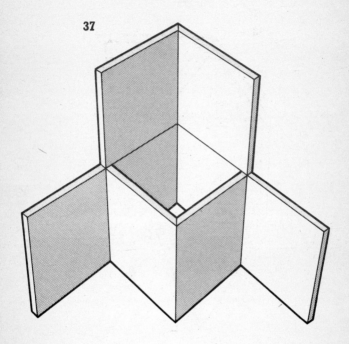

38

39 The big S

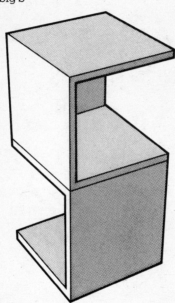

40 Kissing couch

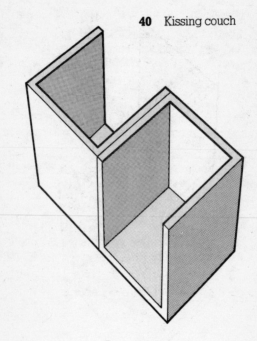

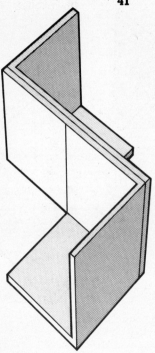

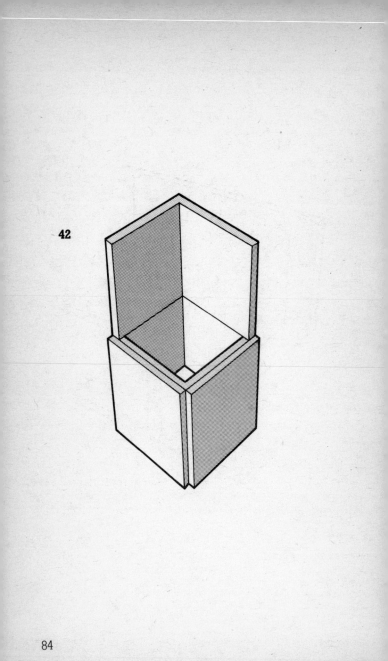

42

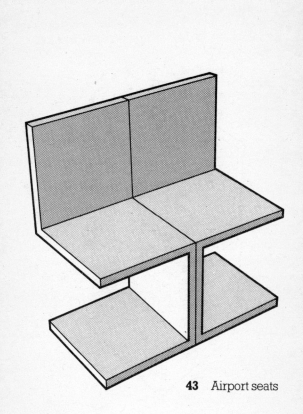

43 Airport seats

44 Pulpit

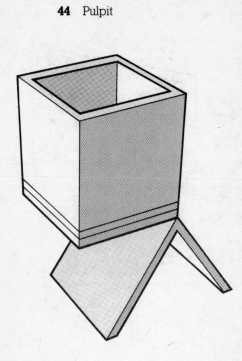

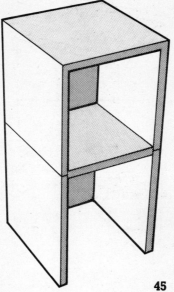

45 Cabinet

46 Six-star

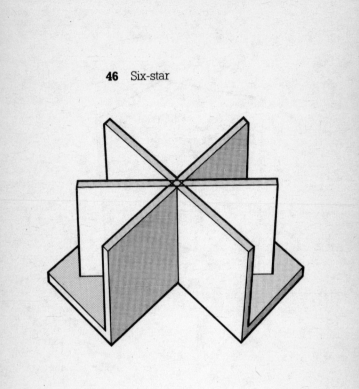

47

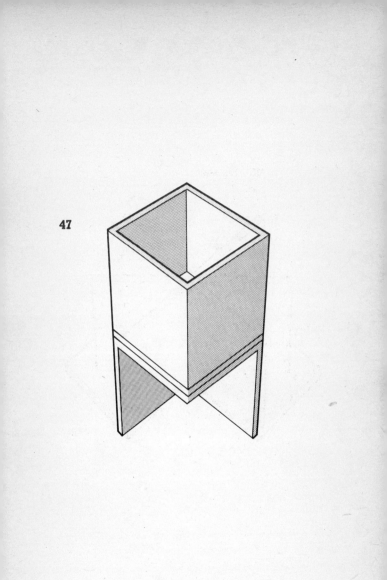

48 Shelf unit

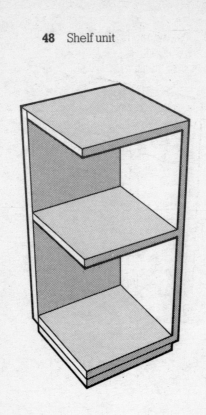

49 Telephone booth

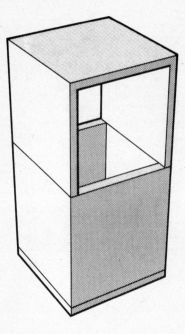

50

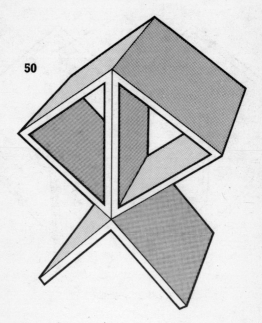

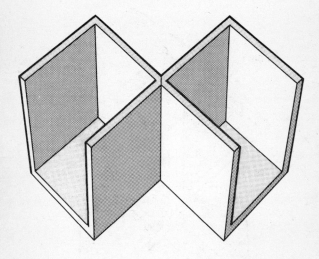

51 Corner seats

52

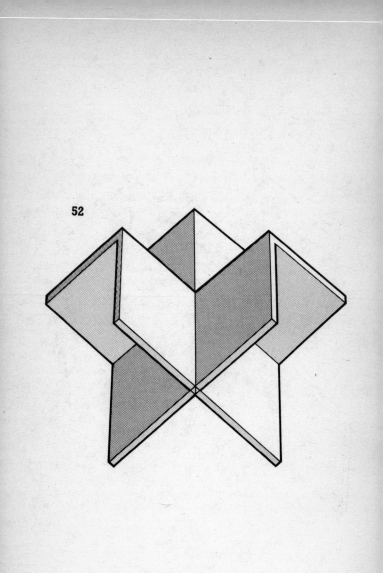

53 Long cross

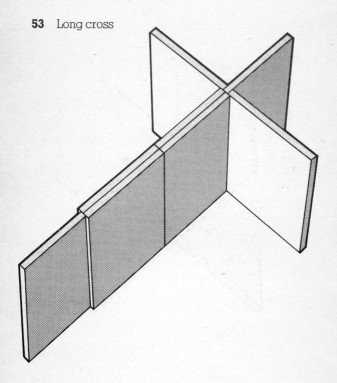

54 The cube

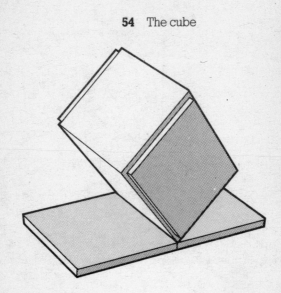